Of Seasons

Gracie Delaney

BookLeaf Publishing

India | USA | UK

Presentation by *BookLeaf Publishing*

Web: www.bookleafpub.com

E-mail: info@bookleafpub.com

ISBN : 9789357447577

First edition 2021

DEDICATION

For you, Ocean Eyes. Thank you for reminding me that there is beauty to be found in each of life's seasons... and thank you for seeing the beauty in me.

Seasons

If all I know of seasons,
it's that time can move so strangely.
Seasons,
they come and go to come
and go again;
time, it runs on with little
feeling.
It has proven difficult to hold;
my hands, they have worn
from the weariness
that comes from failing
to fold the days,
the months and moments of
my own small life into the
four corners of a square
(sides pressed, sides creased,
pressure upon the edges).
Time, I have discovered,
arrives late to healing;
bright colours become grey
and skin fades slow into
dust,
but still I'm sat here praying
that the past might be undone.

And yet, and yet -
if all I know of seasons,
it's that time has earned my patience.
Seasons,
they come and go to come
again with tomorrow;
time, it moves forward so strangely.
Strangely, slowly,
and still
I'll breathe with hope.

Summer

And despite myself,
I chose to love him, then.
In the white-yellow,
in the Summertime,
with the dried grass hot
beneath my feet,
I knew our warmth would fade;
even then,
that bloom of ours sat frail
between my thumbs.
But the beating within my chest
heightened and hummed;
I pressed that bloom
between the pages
of an old prayer book,
and beneath whiskey and weeknights
that I watched wander into
dawn,
I hid those prayers away.
Despite myself,
I swallowed down that Summer;
I drowned myself in a sunlight
that left me red and raw.

Youth

There's a haze within the sky,
tonight.
A warm sort of wind;
the clouds
and the Moon
and all of her little lights
    flutter
        down
through the cracks within
the atmosphere.
Smoke within my lungs,
and the fire we have
piled
and poked
has burned itself behind my eyes.
Tonight,
we'll lay claim to impossibilities
that will never touch
our hands.
Blood and bone,
young bodies not built to last;
between emptied bottles
and sharp-sand dunes,
we'll make love to our
invincibility.

Sunday Morning

Sunday morning,
and I'm alone beside
the bones
of this long-lulled
fire pit:
sitting, singing,
suffocating beneath
the sad stories
that I've sewn for myself.
Sunday morning,
and I wonder:
will he remember the Summer
that made me cry?
Will he remember
how the wind was rough
and warm,
and how his own word-smoke
hazed the air?
Saturday evening,
and I let him call me lover,
his beginning,
his scapegoat,
his end.
Yet this Summer Sunday morning,
I've woken with a heart

too weary
to bend.

Water, Bones

There's little sense to me,
this Summer.
Little standing,
little substance -
only whiskey,
and waves against the rocks.
I'm red,
salt-raw and sun-blown,
and empty:
only water, only bones.

The Impossible

Perhaps,
as our Summer
fluttered
and found itself dimming
into an unfamiliar shade,
those tears I wasted
were not for what was
gone.
Perhaps,
as the warmth was warped
by the wind
and the petals I never did water
curled in towards the dirt,
tears were wasted on
what was never.
What was never, what was not,
what won't ever be.
Because,
perhaps I promised
the impossible.
To see his lips lift in love,
to see that shift in his
willow-bark eyes,
to see him
whole

for a single, ephemeral moment,
well:
perhaps I promised
the impossible.

Autumn

There sits our bloom
between those pages:
brittle, and bruised,
hard pressed.
Seasons shifting,
and my fool heart has
longed for deep-amber-canopy skies.
Yet these clouds hang
grim and grey,
the clouds float low,
this Autumn.
Our bloom between
those pages,
and I never thought
I would mourn
the Summer.

Undertow

And the truth of it is this:
I have loved you
since the Summertime.
For all the ways you watch,
for the way in which you
smile
within those moments
between they and he
and the dimness
and me.
Streetlights against your face,
light upon the lines of you
that lift and lilt -
a tide of ebbing,
exhausted hope.
Speeding along this coastline road,
I'm pulled into your
undertow.
Your eyes like the
darling ocean,
and I have loved you
since the Summer.

As Of Late

I've found myself aching,
as of late:
for the quiet, for the life
and the fragments of myself
that I've long since left behind.
Through the mess,
through the mist upon the windows
of my world,
I watch myself stumbling:
towards tomorrow,
towards a life-of-sorts that feels
heavy between my lungs.
I'm getting tired -
of late nights, and late nights
once again,
and of banter and bullshit
and songs to which
I've never really known the words.
The shadows seem longer,
as of late:
not quite ending, always stretching,
and I'm trapped beneath
a sky that's
ever-sinking.

Nowhere

I find him, waiting -
just as they said he'd be.
He's standing -
(standing, standing)
smoke between his teeth
and the weight of three weeks
apart from me absent;
there's nothing heavy
upon his shoulders.

    'Where have you
     been?'

He smirks
(the faintest tilt of lips)
and offers me a kindness:

    'Nothing, no one,
     nowhere.'

Sometimes

Sometimes, somewhere -
    somewhere between the neon
    and the grey
    and the pulse that beats
    behind my eyes -
I catch a flicker
of a reflection
of myself that wonders:

    'Where will I be when
     this whiskey has
     wasted from my bloodstream?'

When the music becomes
muted and mumbled,
and when the smoke fades
from fog
to wisp
to not-really-there-at-all,
when regret settles sharp
between both lungs:

    'Where will I be when
     this season
     falls

to
earth?'

Winter

Once, I loved the cold.
Grey mornings,
bright-white against the skyline,
bright-white behind my eyes.
Breathing comes in vapour;
as a child, I loved the cold.

But these bones of mine,
they're aching.
Bright-white, and the white
is a sheet and the light
is a bulb that refuses
to flicker out.
I'm here, he's not here,
and you are one thousand
worlds away.

This cold, it's creeping in.
It's pressing against
well-locked glass,
and breathing comes with sharpness.
The ache sits heavy
between my lungs;
it's difficult, breathing alone.

Love

Love,
    I've watched you every day since you
    forgot about me.
    It's not been easy;
    it's not been all that
    difficult.
    Because watching you is like
        breathing
          underwater:
    Painful,
    exquisitely so,
    in that way only voluntary self-destruction
    can be.

Love,
    your oblivion has become the
        centre
      of my orbit.
    the coffees that we
    no longer share
    and the whiskey I swallow down
    alone
    mark my mornings and
    tell me that it's night.

But Love,
    God help me:
    I have loved you as though you are
    so much more
    than a piece of paper
    upon which I'll never
    be permitted
        to write.
    My hands have forgotten
    the words;
    your eyes,
    they have forgotten me altogether.

But Love,
    those eyes:
    they still remind me of the ocean.
    Still water, wild water,
    waters blue and grey.
    And so, I'll keep you here:
    behind the glass of my memory,
    sharp, soft,
            saline and silt.

Love,
    I'll keep you here,
    until the whiskey dries and the
    night
        seeps
            in.

I'll keep you here, then let you
loose:
to lap
and lick
at my fingertips,
and lull me of to sleep.

Pieces

What can I say of myself, then?
That I'm cracking, crumbling?

(You're falling apart.)

That I'm just pieces as apposed
to a whole?

(Not too far from the truth.)

Can I say that I'm any more than
the sum of these dented,
dented parts?

(Can you? Can you
really say?)

And indeed,
I'm made up of wires:
wires of sunlight, wires of atoms
and air,
but the sun seems cold -

(You're getting cold.)

- and my skin feels tight around
my bones.

        (Your fingertips, they're
                slipping.)

I've no more air in these lungs.

The Quiet

And yet,
above all else,
the worst of it is this:
those words,
they left his lips,
but I'd long-since
fallen numb.
Once I called him
    'comfortable' -
but those words brought
a quiet death to that.

Here

Tell me that I'm…
here?

(Here? Are you?)

Am I?
Am I still here?
How long can a person…

(…hover?)

Yes, I suppose.
How long can a person
hover
between
  one space
and
  the next
before they simply… aren't anymore?
Colours begin to seep, I would imagine.

(Colours. They don't last
forever.)

And so, is that how it goes?
Colours seep, noises become slight sounds
and skin cracks far more readily?
I wonder whether or not anyone else
notices.

                              (They don't notice.)

They don't?
I notice.

                              (It's your skin. Of course you
                                                    notice.)

My skin?
It feels borrowed, to me.
My own skin was softer, and brighter.
I remember:
how often would I lift my hand to the daylight,
just to watch that red-orange bloom
about my veins?
Red-orange, and warm;
my own skin was warmer, I think.

                                        (You
think?)

Yes. I think.

(Have I ever
told you
of
manufactured
memories?)

Have you?
Maybe.
But I do remember the warmth.

(You remember
a lot of things,
don't you?)

Yes.
I suppose I do.

Spring

There it is:
the light is
     leaking
         in.
I've not seen it for some time;
white, and warm,
and watching from the crack between
fabric and wood
that these curtains have never
fully managed
to fill.
It's quiet, this daylight -
quiet and careful,
and fearful.
But I find myself
frightened too:

   'I don't want you
    to go.'

It's a frail thing, this daylight;
I'm holding my breath
as it edges across the room.
Edging through the dust,
edging over the skin

upon my arms that still feels
bloody and broken.
And this daylight,
it's edging across your face:
you,
here and now,
watching me from the edge of the bed.
I'm frightened,
but the light is
        leaking
                in.
This daylight has found your eyes:

    'I promise you
     that I'll stay.'

Bottles

We sit, together,
you and me,
peering at the world through
a warm-brown glass.
Whiskey and wit,
caffeine, night-air nicotine:
I'll hold your hand,
and you'll unlace the
    tangle
       of
     my
        thoughts.

It's a strange thing,
this friendship.
An oddity:
a buzzing in our blood
tugging us to whisper,
to wonder,
to settle in the safety
that is born from
    no one else around.

You're here and I'm here,
and we're lining up

our paradigms
like bottles:
half-emptied, half-full,
never quite meeting but
half of you
          and
          half of me,
all the same.

It's a strange thing,
this friendship -
a fractured thing, a
tiny
broken
miracle.

Boxes

And so,
all that I've been
sits boxed about
my knees:
corners,
and edges,
and seams sealed shut
with brown-yellow tape.
Four years,
and perhaps I expected
a torrent.
And yet,
all that I've been
sits boxed about
my ankles:
corners,
and memories,
and the dust of
settling peace.

Constellations

And so,
I'll carry these marks
upon the soft of my arms:
white-pink keloid,
flints of yesterday
threaded beneath my skin.
Sometimes,
when the clouds hang ever too
heavy and the air
wraps its warmth about my throat,
I'll let you trace those edges.
With your fingers,
you'll weave constellations -
your touch cradles
these weary veins.

Ocean Eyes

Blue, and grey,
and somewhere in between;
my Love, I have always called you
'Ocean'.
For all your crashing, for all your tides,
in your undertow,
at last,
I'm home.